Ancient Roman

W

W

Brian W.

MAIDSTONE

NOV   6-4-19

15. OCT

13. DEC

– 2 NOV 2009

2 5 FEB 2012

– 4 MAY 2012

KT-479-425

Books should be returned or renewed by the
last date stamped above.

Kent
County
Council

CHARTER
MARK

CUSTOMER SERVICE EXCELLENCE

00884\DTP\R N\04.05   LIB 7

C152689614

www.heinemann.co.uk/library
Visit our website to find out more information about **Heinemann Library** books.

To order:

☎ Phone 44 (0) 1865 888066

▤ Send a fax to 44 (0) 1865 314091

▭ Visit the Heinemann Bookshop at www.heinemann.co.uk/library to browse our catalogue and order online.

First published in Great Britain by Heinemann Library, Halley Court, Jordan Hill, Oxford OX2 8EJ, part of Harcourt Education. Heinemann is a registered trademark of Harcourt Education Ltd.

© Harcourt Education Ltd 2002.
First published in paperback 2003

The moral right of the proprietor has been asserted.

All rights reserved. No part of this publication may be reproduced, stored in a retrieval system, or transmitted in any form or by any means, electronic, mechanical, photocopying, recording, or otherwise without either the prior written permission of the Publishers or a licence permitting restricted copying in the United Kingdom issued by the Copyright Licensing Agency Ltd, 90 Tottenham Court Road, London W1P 0LP.

Designed by Tinstar Design (www.tinstar.co.uk)
Illustrated by Jeff Edwards
Originated by Ambassador Litho Ltd
Printed in China by Wing King Tong

ISBN 0 431 145 601 (hardback)   ISBN 0 431 145 652 (paperback)
06 05 04 03 02   07 06 05 04 03
10 9 8 7 6 5 4 3 2 1   10 9 8 7 6 5 4 3 2 1

British Library Cataloguing in Publication Data
Williams, Brian
     Ancient Roman war and weapons. – (People in the past)
     1. Military art and science – Rome – History – Juvenile literature
     2. Weapons, Ancient – Rome – Juvenile literature
     3. Civilization, Modern – Roman influences – Juvenile literature
     4. Rome – Social conditions – 510–30 B.C. – Juvenile literature
     I.Title
     355'.02'0937

Acknowledgements
The Publishers would like to thank the following for permission to reproduce photographs:
AKG Photos, London p8 (National Museum of Archaeology, Naples), 12 (Kunsthistorishes Museum, Vienna/ Erich Lessing), 20 (Hilbich), 6, 22 (Erich Lessing), 30 (Michael Telier), 34 (Vatican Museum, Rome); Ancient Art & Architecture Collection pp7, 13, 14, 16, 21, 24, 26, 28, 29, 31, 32, 36, 42; Art Archive p 40; Bridgeman Art Library p10; Scala Art Resource p23; Terry Griffiths & Magnet Harlequin pp18, 19, 43; Trevor Clifford p38.

Cover photograph reproduced with permission of AKG London.

Every effort has been made to contact copyright holders of any material reproduced in this book. Any omissions will be rectified in subsequent printings if notice is given to the Publisher.

KENT
ARTS & LIBRARIES

C152689614

J355.00937

Contents

Words appearing in the text in bold, **like this**, are explained in the Glossary.

Who were the Romans?

From the hills of northern Britain to the deserts of the Middle East, Roman armies stood guard two thousand years ago. Roman soldiers conquered and then defended Rome's **empire**. The sight and sound of these warriors tramping into battle struck fear into most of the peoples of Europe, North Africa and western Asia.

The Romans' story began, according to their own history books, in 753 BC. For almost 500 years they ruled one of the great empires of history, thanks to their well-trained soldiers and their formidable weapons. In this book, you will discover what these soldiers were like – how they lived, how they trained, what weapons they had and how they fought. You will also find out that the Roman soldier was a builder as well as a fighter, who left his mark wherever he marched and made his home.

The Romans' homeland was Italy. Their city of Rome became the centre of the Roman Empire. Rome was a city of great buildings: temples, palaces, arenas, and monuments to Rome's soldiers. The most interesting army monument that still survives today is Trajan's Column, a stone pillar on which is carved a 'picture-strip' story of Roman soldiers at war. Here we can see in detail soldiers of the **Emperor** Trajan as they fight and conquer Dacia (modern Romania). It is a remarkable record.

Not all Roman soldiers, however, came from Italy. The Roman army included soldiers from many lands, with different languages and religions, who became part of the Roman Empire. Wherever they fought and conquered, these soldiers built roads and towns. The remains of some Roman buildings can still be seen, while more lies buried beneath the streets and squares of modern cities.

The first Romans were farmers, not warriors. They lived in thatched huts built on seven hills beside the River Tiber in a region called Latium in central Italy. Roman children were taught that their city had been founded by twin brothers named Romulus and Remus, who were raised by a she-wolf. Every Roman knew the story.

Another story told of a soldier's bravery. In the 600s BC the Romans fell under the rule of the **Etruscans**, but around 510 BC they revolted and drove out their Etruscan king, Tarquin the Proud. An army of Etruscans and mercenaries attacked Rome, led by a **general** named Lars Porsena. So began one of the most famous stories of Roman soldiering – the stand by Horatius on the bridge.

The Roman Empire was at its biggest in about AD 100. It stretched from Britain, in the west, to Egypt and Mesopotamia (modern Turkey/Iraq), in the east.

Horatius and the bridge

General Lars Porsena's men rushed to cross the bridge over the River Tiber, beyond which lay Rome. Three Romans, Horatius and two companions, ran onto the narrow wooden bridge, and the fight began. As the three fought bravely, other Romans hacked at the bridge with axes. Finally, Horatius told his friends to save themselves, and as the bridge collapsed, he leapt into the river. One story says he was drowned, but another says he swam ashore and was rewarded with as much land as he could plough in a single day. Brave and loyal to his friends, Horatius was the kind of hero Roman soldiers loved.

Warrior republic

For almost 500 years the city-state of Rome was a **republic**. Its people were called **citizens** of Rome, and they were expected to fight to defend the republic. They were part-time soldiers. After fighting, men went back to their farms.

Learning from enemies

The early Romans fought other peoples of Italy, such as the Samnites and **Etruscans**. Often their enemies had better weapons. The Romans copied the best weapons and tactics, and learned from their defeats. After the attack by Lars Porsena's army, they joined forces with **allies**, including people from Cumae, a Greek settlement near Naples, and in the end the Etruscans were defeated. With the Etruscans beaten, Rome became the strongest of Italy's city-states.

Most Romans fought on foot, but they learned to fight enemies such as the Campanians, who fought on horseback, and the **Celts** who drove horse-drawn chariots.

This is a Roman carving of a Celtic war chariot, pulled by two horses. Across Europe, the Celts fought many battles against the Romans.

In 390 BC, an army of Celts called **Gauls** attacked the walled city of Rome itself. One dark night Celtic raiders climbed the Capitoline Hill, but as they scrambled up the wall, the geese that were kept in the Temple of Juno began cackling. The birds woke the Romans just in time to drive off the enemy. To the Romans, this was a sign that the gods were protecting them.

Defeat teaches a lesson

The Battle of the Caudine Forks in 321 BC taught the Romans a lesson. Their army marched into the Samnites' mountain homeland (near Naples), but foolishly failed to send out **scouts**. The Samnites captured the entire Roman army. The Romans were allowed to go home, but only after handing over their weapons. They had to creep under an arch of spears while the Samnites jeered at them.

A Celt would often challenge an enemy to single combat. A Roman soldier who won such a fight became a hero among his comrades. If he lost, his head was put on show in a Celtic temple!

Early Roman weapons

The first Roman soldiers went into battle wearing little armour. Each man wore a helmet and breast-plate made of bronze. They carried bronze shields. Spears, javelins (throwing spears), swords, and axes were also made of bronze.

Bronze weapons were **cast** into shape, by pouring the hot melted metal into a mould. They were sharp, but snapped easily. Casting iron was difficult, because greater heat was required, so an iron sword had to be beaten into shape with a hammer. It was hard work, but the finished sword was much stronger than a bronze weapon – and more precious.

This bronze figure of a Samnite warrior shows the kind of armoured soldier the early Romans fought and beat.

Wars of conquest

The Romans began to believe that the gods meant them to rule other peoples. They defeated the **Etruscans** in the north of Italy and the Greeks, who had settled in towns in the south. The Roman **legion** was becoming an impressive military force, well armed and well disciplined.

Pyrrhic victory

In 280 BC, the Roman soldiers fought for the first time the much feared Greek **phalanx** – a formation of men with long spears. In a bloody battle at Heraclea (a Greek town in Italy), a Greek army led by Pyrrhus beat the Romans.

Yet Pyrrhus lost so many men that 'a Pyrrhic victory' came to mean any victory won at too high a cost. Two years later the Heracleans were under Roman rule.

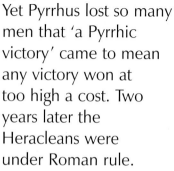

Hannibal of Carthage was the son of a general named Hamilcar Barca, who was beaten by the Romans. Taught by his father to seek revenge, he became commander of the Carthaginian army at the age of 26. His daring attack on Italy almost toppled the might of Rome.

Wars against Carthage

Later, the Romans fought three wars against the people of Carthage, a city in North Africa. These wars are called the Punic Wars, because the Romans used the name 'Punic' to describe the first people who settled in Carthage. The Carthaginians even dared to invade Italy, but by 146 BC, Rome had beaten Carthage, and had won control of Spain and North Africa.

Hannibal's challenge

Hannibal of Carthage was a brilliant general. He surprised the Romans by leading his army across the **Alps** (mountains to the north of Italy) to attack Italy. Even more of a shock were his African war-elephants, trained to charge terrified foot-soldiers and scare **cavalry** horses. Fortunately for the Romans, Hannibal did not have many elephants.

Hannibal led his army of Africans, **Celts** and Spaniards with great skill, until the Roman navy cut off his supplies. A good Roman **general**, Scipio 'the African', attacked Carthage, forcing Hannibal to leave Italy and return to Africa. At the battle of Zama (Tunisia) in 202 BC, Hannibal's army was beaten, after the Romans hired thousands of Hannibal's own African cavalry. Hannibal fled into exile and in 183 BC he killed himself rather than surrendering to Rome.

The Battle of Cannae

The Romans learned hard lessons from Hannibal. In 216 BC, he beat them at the battle of Cannae in southern Italy. The Romans had a huge army of over 80,000 men, but two generals who took daily turns to give orders! This was not a good idea. The Roman **infantry** advanced deep into the lines of Carthaginians, who fell back calmly. Hannibal's cavalry then galloped in on either side, to close the trap. Among the more than 56,000 Roman dead was General Paullus. The other general, Varro, escaped. The Romans blamed him, not his men, for the disaster.

Revolt of the slaves

The Roman army became so strong that ambitious leaders tried to use it to win power. In 82 BC, a **general** named Sulla used his soldiers as a private army, and rival politicians also raised armies. This led to **civil war**.

The revolt of Spartacus

These quarrels weakened Rome, and ten years later a revolt came that for a time seemed to threaten law and order. The revolt of 73–71 BC was an uprising of slaves against their masters. The powerful landowners that ruled Rome forgot their quarrels and joined forces to fight the slave-army.

The slaves' leader, Spartacus, came from Thrace (a country roughly where Greece and Bulgaria are today). He had been a soldier, but later trained as a gladiator. Gladiators were trained to fight, and die, in brutal shows. Crowds filled the Roman arenas to watch gladiators fight one another. A few gladiators became rich and famous, but most were soon killed. Most gladiators were criminals, prisoners of war or slaves.

The gladiator army

Spartacus used his training to make a dash for freedom. With about 70 companions, he broke out of the gladiator school near Naples. Escaping to the slopes of the volcano Vesuvius, the gladiators were joined by runaway slaves, until Spartacus commanded an army of several thousand men.

This amphitheatre, built in Capua, Italy, in 1st century BC, was the second largest in the world. It was where Spartacus led the gladiators to their famous revolt.

This Roman mosaic shows gladiators fighting. Some gladiators had shields and armour, others fought practically naked.

The slave-army moved quickly across country, fed by friendly farmers. The gladiators knew many fighting tricks, which they taught to the slaves and poor people who joined them. They beat the Roman armies sent to hunt them down, and gained more weapons and new recruits. Spartacus planned to march north, to cross the **Alps** so that his men (many of whom were **Gauls** and Germans) could find their way home. However, most of the soldiers were scared and wanted to stay in Italy. So Spartacus turned south, hoping to cross in ships to the island of Sicily, and then to escape across the Mediterranean Sea.

A terrible punishment

The government in Rome sent two generals, Crassus and Pompey, with eight legions (as many as 40,000 men) to hunt down the rebels. There were two fierce battles, and in the second, Spartacus was killed. Many slave-soldiers were killed trying to run away. Thousands more were captured and **crucified** along the road leading to Rome, as a warning to other slaves.

The end for Crassus

Crassus became one of three rulers of Rome, along with Pompey and Julius Caesar. In 54 BC, he invaded Mesopotamia (modern Turkey/Iraq). Crossing the desert, his army was attacked by a fierce people called Parthians, who encircled the Romans with 1000 armoured **cavalry** and 10,000 archers on horseback. The Romans formed a square, sheltering from the Parthian arrows behind their shields, but there was no escape. Trains of camels carried drinking water and more arrows to the Parthian archers, while the Romans fell one by one. At this battle of Carrhae, Crassus was killed and so were more than 30,000 of his men.

Imperial legions

◄▷ ◄▷ ◄▷ ◄▷ ◄▷ ◄▷ ◄▷ ◄▷ ◄▷ ◄▷ ◄▷ ◄▷ ◄▷ ◄▷ ◄▷ ◄▷

The **legion** was the backbone of the Roman army. It was like a regiment in a modern army, with about 5000 soldiers. The legionaries were the best soldiers Rome had, and they were all Roman **citizens**. Each legion had its proud traditions, and its treasured battle honours. Defeat – such as the terrible massacre of three legions by Germans in the Teutoberg Forest in AD 9 – was a disgrace.

How the legion was organized

Like a modern regiment, a legion had a name and number – such as Second Augusta. In the time of the first Roman **emperor** Augustus (after whom this legion was named), there were 28 legions. Earlier in Roman history, there were twice as many.

Each legion was commanded by a **legate**, who was often the governor of a **province**. Under him were young officers called tribunes. The legion had its office staff, such as clerks to write out orders, messengers and a medical unit.

The legion was divided into ten smaller units called cohorts, usually about 500 strong, although the First Cohort, which was the best, was twice that size. The First Cohort guarded the legion's gold eagle, or aquila. In each cohort, there were six centuries, of 80 to 100 men, under the command of a **centurion**.

A carved figure of a standard-bearer, carrying the legion's eagle. The eagle standard was the most treasured symbol in the Roman army, carried into battle at the head of the legion.

The tombstone of Marcus Favonius Facilis, a centurion who served with the 20th Legion in Britain. The legion was based for a time at Colchester, after helping to capture the city from the Britons in AD 43, and his memorial stone was found there. Notice his stick and sword, worn on the left.

Centurions and standard-bearers

A centurion's rank was roughly the same as a sergeant in a modern army, but some centurions were more important than others. A senior centurion commanded the First Cohort. A centurion wore a special uniform with decorations (his medals), ornamented belt and cloak, and he wore his sword on the left side. He also carried a stick. A picture of a centurion named Marcus Favonius Facilis is carved on his tombstone at Colchester, England. Senior centurions ran army camps, and were in charge of equipment and transport.

Standard-bearers wore a lion-skin or bear-skin headdress. They marched at the head of the men. Trumpeters blew long, curling trumpets as the troops advanced to battle.

Standards and flags

The legion's standards were held high on poles, so that in the confusion and dust of battle everyone could see them. They were also important religious symbols, kept in a special shrine, sacred to the gods, in the legion's fort or base camp. When the legion left camp, so did its gold eagle standard and for a legion to lose its eagle to an enemy was thought a terrible disgrace. Legions also carried a standard bearing a picture of the emperor. Each century in a legion had its own standard, called a *signum*, and also small flags called *vexilla*.

Special forces

Just like a modern army, the Roman army had special forces for special tasks. Many of these soldiers were **auxiliaries**. They were not Romans, but warriors recruited from other lands, with their own skills and favourite weapons.

Cavalrymen from Africa

Among the best troops in the Roman army were Numidian horsemen. These cavalrymen came from the part of North Africa that is now Algeria. They were superb riders, riding bareback from boyhood, rather like the Comanches of North America or the Mongols of Asia.

Soldiers of the Praetorian guard wore distinctive helmets and carried oval shields. There were over 4500 men in this guard, under one commander, who was often the most powerful man in Rome, after the emperor.

Sling-shooters

The sling was an ancient throwing weapon. It was a long strip of leather or cloth. A stone was placed in the middle and holding both ends of the sling, the soldier whirled it around. When he let go of one end, the stone flew out at high speed. A barrage of well-aimed stones could be as effective as a shower of arrows. The best slingers came from the Balearic Islands off the coast of Spain, and from the Middle East. They wore little armour, and could move fast and hide behind rocks and bushes.

The Numidians would fight for whoever paid them the most. During Rome's wars against Carthage (see pages 8–9), the Roman **general** Scipio bribed the Numidians in Hannibal's army to change sides. The Numidians wore no armour, and so could be shot down by massed **infantry**, but they were deadly in 'hit and run' attacks, and for pursuing fleeing enemies. On Trajan's Column, Numidian horsemen are shown chasing defeated Dacians.

Archers and slingers

The best archers in the Roman army came from Crete and Syria, and shot arrows from powerful composite (double-bent) bows. There is a tombstone of a Syrian archer at Housesteads Fort on Hadrian's Wall in Britain, the most northerly part of the **Empire**. He was a long way from home. As well as arrows, soldiers also hurled stones (see box).

Bodyguards and swordsmen

Defeated enemies often joined the army of their conquerors. Celtic warriors, admired by Romans because they were so tall, guarded the **emperors**. The Praetorian Guard was formed by the emperor Augustus. Soldiers in the Guard were paid three times as much as a **legionary** and wore old-fashioned uniforms, with oval shields.

The Romans also recruited Spanish swordsmen. These soldiers preferred a curved 'slashing' sword to the short 'stabbing' sword favoured by the Romans. Spanish soldiers were also feared for throwing wicked-looking javelins with barbed tips, like fishing spears.

Cavalry

The Romans preferred to fight on foot. In the early days of the Roman **Republic**, only nobles fought on horseback. But every legion in the **empire** had its **cavalry**. Horse-soldiers were usually foreign troops or **auxiliaries**, and in the later years of the Empire, more cavalry soldiers were used as the Romans struggled to fight off raiding enemies.

Cavalry in war

When they first came to Britain, Roman soldiers were impressed and scared by the **Celts** dashing into their ranks in horse-drawn chariots. War chariots had gone out of fashion in Italy, and the Romans used chariots only for transport and races. They also admired the speed and power of the German-Celtic horse-soldiers with whom they fought frontier battles along the Rhine and Danube rivers.

To fight these enemies, the Romans recruited horsemen, such as Thracians from the Black Sea region of Eastern Europe, and Numidians from North Africa.

The tombstone of a Roman cavalryman, found in Gloucester, England. The writing, in Latin, tells us that his name was Rufus Sita, and that his regiment came originally from Thrace. He is shown using his long lance against a fallen enemy.

A German horseman often fought alongside a foot-soldier, the man on foot running beside the horse. The Romans used these tough Germans as 'commandos', for surprise attacks, often sending raiding parties across rivers at night to catch the enemy sleeping.

Cavalry show-offs

Cavalry soldiers enjoyed showing off on the training ground. Riders competed in contests to show off their skill with sword and lance. They wore decorated gold and bronze sports armour, with fancy helmets covering the wearer's face.

In a battle, the cavalry rode on either side of the army, to protect the mass of **infantry** in the centre. A general sent his orders by a galloping horseman. When the enemy army broke under the steady push of the **legions**, the cavalry charged in to scatter them and complete the victory.

Cavalry arms and armour

From pictures on tombstones and monuments, we know that Roman cavalrymen wore **mail** shirts. They had long swords, known as spathas, copied from the long swords used by the Celts. They also carried a lance, or long spear. Even without stirrups (not yet used in the West), a rider was held firmly in his seat by the high Roman saddle. The cavalryman's shield was carried strapped to his horse's flank until he went into battle.

By the AD 300s, the Romans were using heavier armoured cavalry to fight off growing hordes of **barbarian** invaders. Called *cataphracts*, these soldiers wore armour coats made of mail reaching down to the knee, with a hood covering the head. Armoured coats also protected cavalry horses. The cataphract fought with a long lance and sword. Knocked from his horse, however, this heavy soldier was often helpless against a quick, lightly armed opponent. His mail shirt alone weighed 30 kilograms, so the soldier wearing it had to be very strong.

The Roman soldier

The Roman soldier was trained to obey orders and to help his comrades. Training was tough. In return, he was well paid and generally looked after.

Learning to be a legionary

A new recruit did marching **drill** twice a day, and three times a month had to complete a 29-kilometre cross-country march. He became fit enough to march at 7 kilometres an hour. Each soldier learnt to march in a column (narrow line), and change to long lines ready for battle. He also learnt to keep a tidy camp. Every Roman soldier knew how to pitch a tent, how to dig latrines (toilets), and how to build a fort.

In weapons training, soldiers practised with a wooden sword and a basketwork shield, each twice as heavy as the real thing. This helped strengthen muscles, and in a battle, made a real sword and shield feel quite light and easy to use. In mock battles, soldiers used swords and spears with blunted points. They swam across rivers in full kit, holding on to blown-up animal-skins. They learned to leap onto a horse, wearing full armour, and to ride without stirrups.

From the remains of Roman forts, like Housesteads on Hadrian's Wall in northern England, **archaeologists** can work out how Roman soldiers lived in barracks. This headquarters building contained offices, a strongroom (for money and treasure) and an armoury (for weapons).

This grindstone would have been the upper of two stones. As it was turned by a handle, grain was poured in through the hole, and crushed between the two stones so flour trickled out around the sides. Big grindstones like this one, found not far from Hadrian's Wall (and now in Corbridge Museum), would have been too heavy to carry, so soldiers would also have had small portable grindstones.

The tales told by old soldiers warned the young recruits about strange and frightening foes! In battle, the Romans might face trumpeting war-elephants, Celtic charioteers who fought stark naked or Parthian archers who shot arrows as a 'parting shot' while galloping away on horseback.

The life of a soldier

Weapons, clothes, and food were supplied, but the cost was taken away from a soldier's pay. Any soldier belonging to a **legion** had to be a Roman **citizen**. He earned three times as much as an **auxiliary**, who was not a citizen. Auxiliaries could become citizens after 25 years' army service.

The Roman soldier fought hard, and often fought far from his home country. Victory, or a new **emperor**, meant extra pay, however, and on retirement he was given money to help him settle down to **civilian** life, as a farmer in a **veterans'** settlement. Each soldier paid money into a burial fund, to pay for his funeral and a headstone.

Barracks life

Roman soldiers lived in **barracks**, just like many soldiers today. Eight men shared a tent or a barrack room. They also shared a **mule**, to carry their tent and a millstone for grinding corn. All soldiers had to do routine jobs such as cleaning toilets and tidying up the barracks, except those with special skills, like blacksmiths or fletchers (arrow-makers).

Armour and weapons

Much of what we know about Roman armour and weapons comes from pictures and carvings like those on Trajan's Column in Rome. Metal is not often preserved after 2000 years, but pieces of armour, rusted weapons and helmets are found by **archaeologists** at military sites, such as Hadrian's Wall in Britain.

To protect his head, a Roman soldier wore a metal helmet, with neck guard and cheek plates. He wore chest and shoulder armour made of strips of iron, held together with hinges and leather straps. A small apron made of metal discs hung from his belt.

The sword

From the belt also hung a sword, in a **scabbard**, and a dagger. The Roman sword was short, and was used to stab at the enemy. Longer swords, with slashing edges, were used by other warriors, but the **legionaries** preferred their short swords. At first legionaries wore their swords on the right. Only **centurions** and eagle **standard** bearers wore their swords on the left. By the AD 300s though, most Roman soldiers wore their swords on the left side.

A **Celt** would whirl his sword high in the air, then chop down with it. This looked terrifying, but the Roman soldier was trained to take the blow on the rim of his shield. Sometimes the enemy's sword snapped. Keeping low behind his shield, the Roman would then thrust his own sword into his enemy.

In this scene, carved in relief on Trajan's Column, some Roman soldiers battle against enemy warriors, while others build defences.

Here are some examples of Roman swords and scabbards. The short stabbing sword was the legionaries' traditional weapon. The longer sword slowly replaced it in the AD 200s.

The javelin

In battle, a **legion** advanced in line. As they got near the enemy, the men threw their javelins. The javelin was a long wooden spear with a thin iron shaft. The point was hard, but the shaft bent easily. If the javelin did not kill an enemy soldier, it stuck awkwardly in his shield. Being bent, it could not be flung back. Each soldier carried two javelins. After throwing their javelins, the Romans charged, stabbing with their swords.

The shield

A shield helped protect the soldier. The legionary shield was a curved rectangle, which enclosed the front of the soldier's body. It was made of thin sheets of wood stuck together and covered with leather. The rim and the centrepiece (boss) were made of iron. **Cavalry** and **auxiliaries** carried oval shields, and by about AD 200 flat oval shields became more or less standard for all Romans.

Mons Graupius AD 84

Roman training was usually enough to beat less disciplined opponents. Mons Graupius was a battle fought in Caledonia (modern Scotland), during the Roman conquest of Britain. The Roman **general** Agricola led the lines of legionaries up a hill, the Romans keeping behind their shields. When the enemy charged in their chariots, they were driven off by Roman cavalry. The Romans said they killed over 10,000 Britons in this battle, for the loss of only 400 of their own men.

On the march

The Roman army travelled on foot, building roads as it went. On the march, every **legionary** soldier carried his kit slung from a pole resting on his shoulder. Packed into leather bags were his spare clothes (woollen **tunic** and short trousers, socks in cold weather), personal belongings, food dish, cooking pot and rations for three days. Soldiers lived on bread, porridge, bacon fat, soup, cheese and vegetables, plus any fruit or fresh meat they could find.

Each man carried his weapons, helmet, shield and tools – saw, pick, axe, billhook (for cutting branches), a basket and a length of chain. A Roman soldier was very fit! The men marched for 5-6 hours a day, covering about 30 kilometres before halting to make camp for the night.

Making camp

Engineers went on ahead to pick a good camp site, level the ground and mark out the edges of a rectangle. When the main force arrived, the men stripped off their marching kit, and started digging ditches around the camp, piling up soil and turf to make a dirt wall on the inside.

Then the soldiers set up tents – officers' in the centre, men's tents in straight lines around. The leather tents looked like the ridge tents used by campers today.

Roman roads were used long after the Romans had abandoned countries. This is all that remains of the Lechaion Road in Corinth, Greece. Some modern roads follow the routes planned and laid by Roman army road-builders.

In this scene from Trajan's Column, Roman legionary soldiers are marching through a town.

Road and bridges

Roman roads were built by the army for the army, though other travellers were also glad of them. **Surveyors** mapped the path of a new road, in as straight a line as possible. Soldiers dug out the road bed and laid stones to make a hardwearing surface. Some Roman roads were still in use a thousand years later.

The Romans also built bridges. Julius Caesar's army built a wooden bridge across the River Rhine in Germany in just ten days. The army marched over to show the Germans how strong Rome was. Having made their point, the Romans then marched back again, and destroyed the bridge.

Standing on your own feet

The Roman military boot, or *caliga*, was like a sandal. It was cut from a single strip of leather, and had a thick leather sole shod with iron studs, hardwearing but slippery. The **historian** Josephus watched a Roman **centurion** run across a paved courtyard, and fall over when his studs slipped on the smooth stones.

The army abroad

Some of what we know about the Roman army at war comes from what the Romans wrote. Other information is found on tombstones, letters and monuments like Trajan's Column. The **general** Julius Caesar wrote about his wars outside Italy, in **Gaul** and in Britain, and about the different peoples his armies fought.

The Romans abroad

The Romans fought to gain more land, and to defend their **frontiers** against 'outsiders', whom they called **barbarians**. The people they conquered became part of the Roman world. Sometimes Roman armies invaded by sea, as when they conquered Britain. More often, armies marched overland, building roads and forts as they went. Sometimes the Romans made **treaties** with friendly rulers, to get what they wanted without fighting.

Julius Caesar made his name as a soldier by conquering Gaul, where he lost only two battles. He led by example, marching with his men, swimming rivers, and often dashing on ahead in a chariot, so fast that he arrived at the next camp before the messengers sent to warn the soldiers the general was coming!

This is a statue of Julius Caesar. Coming from a noble family, he won fame as a soldier and became the most powerful man in Rome.

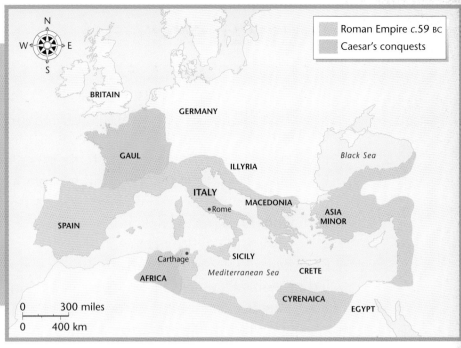

This map shows the lands conquered by Julius Caesar by c.59 BC. His army captured Gaul after a nine-year campaign that began in 58 BC. He twice crossed the River Rhine to frighten the Germans, and invaded Britain twice, in 55 and 54 BC.

How to win battles

Caesar was fond of springing surprises, such as turning out the troops to parade in the pouring rain. Before a battle, he would tell his soldiers that every rumour about the enemy was true, so 'you may as well stop asking questions and making guesses'. The message was clear: stop talking, stop worrying, and win the battle!

Intelligence (information) could be the key to victory. Before marching into unfamiliar territory, a good general made sure the army was safe from **ambush** by sending out **scouts**. He also won the respect of his men. Caesar's men liked him because he called them 'Comrades', rather than treating them as inferiors, and because he doubled their pay. Caesar insisted on smartness. If a soldier were rewarded with a silver-decorated sword, then surely he would fight all the harder to keep it.

Julius Caesar

Julius Caesar is the most famous Roman of all. He was a politician turned soldier. During Rome's civil wars, he disobeyed an order to give up his army and instead led over 5000 men across the Rubicon, a river separating the territory he governed from the rest of Italy. His boldness paid off. He later beat his rival Pompey in a battle at Pharsalus in Greece. This made Caesar so powerful that he might have become king of Rome, had he not been murdered in 44 BC.

The invaders

Until AD 43, Britain was just outside the Roman world. Its people were tribes of **Celts**, each with its own king. Julius Caesar had landed twice, but not stayed. Some British tribes traded with the Roman world and Britain was rich, so in AD 43 the **emperor** Claudius decided the island would be a good prize. He wanted to win a victory, and he also wanted to keep his **generals** busy – so they would not plot against him.

Claudius told the army to invade Britain. Forty thousand soldiers, led by Aulus Plautius, crossed the Channel in ships and landed in Kent. **Auxiliaries** swam the River Medway to attack the British chariots, while the **legionaries** waded across a shallow place in the river. The Romans defeated the British leader Caratacus, who fled west into Wales.

The Romans took control of the important cities of Camulodunum (modern Colchester) and Londinium (London). One **legion** stayed in Colchester, two others moved north, while a fourth marched west. Caratacus was again defeated and this time taken as a captive to Rome. The Romans began building roads and forts, to control their new **province**.

Storming Maiden Castle

In AD 43, the year of the invasion, the Second Legion captured the **hill-fort** of Maiden Castle, in Dorset. On this great earth mound, ringed by ditches, the British must have felt safe. Then the Romans attacked fiercely, their catapults bombarding the fort with stones and giant arrows. Many defenders – men, women and children – died during the fighting. The victorious Roman commander, Vespasian, later became emperor.

Boudicca's revolt

In AD 60, the Iceni tribe of eastern Britain rose in revolt, led by their queen Boudicca (see left). The great new Roman temple in Colchester was destroyed, and the rebels swept down on London, where they killed over 70,000 people. Dead bodies and weapons were thrown into the River Thames – even today bones and rusted iron swords are still found in the mud. A layer of red burned clay beneath the modern city shows how fierce was the fire that destroyed Roman London.

The Roman governor Suetonius Paulinus reorganized his legions and the Romans fought the rebels somewhere north of London. Boudicca commanded over 120,000 warriors, who fought bravely, but the legions stood their ground, in tight ranks. By the end of the day, the enemy had fled, leaving (the Romans said) 80,000 dead. Queen Boudicca swallowed poison rather than be taken prisoner.

This statue of Queen Boudicca in her chariot stands in London, beside the River Thames. The Roman **historian** Dio Cassius (writing about 150 years after her death) described the warrior-queen as 'very tall and grim', with a sharp gaze, harsh voice and reddish hair so long it reached her hips.

Siege warfare

The Romans were good engineers, as well as good soldiers. Their skills at making machines came in useful when attacking a fortress or a city with high stone walls. In a **siege** of a town or fort, soldiers tried to climb over the walls, knock holes in them or dig beneath them. Sometimes, the Romans built walls to trap an enemy. Julius Caesar did this when he surrounded the town of Alesia in **Gaul** in 52 BC. His engineers trapped one army of Gauls inside rings of stakes, spikes and ditches, leaving the Roman soldiers free to fight a second, even bigger enemy army.

War engines

The Romans had two main kinds of **artillery** for throwing **missiles**. The biggest was the catapult, or *onager*. This machine had a long arm held in thick twisted cords, with a spoon-shaped end to hold the missile. To fire the catapult, soldiers pulled back the arm with a **winch**, twisting the cords tighter and tighter. When the arm was released, it shot forwards and flung a rock or a lump of burning tar as far as 300 metres.

The *ballista* looked like a giant crossbow. It was fired by two soldiers, turning winch-wheels to draw back the bow string and release a big dart-like arrow called a bolt. Some ballistas could be loaded with a number of bolts, which were fired automatically, one after the other. By the AD 300s every Roman **legion** went to battle with 10 catapults and 60 *ballistas*.

Here, a replica of a Roman *ballista* is shown. This powerful and accurate spring-gun could be moved on a cart pulled by mules or oxen. It was also useful for firing from siege towers or from fortress walls.

Bringing down the walls

In 49 BC, Julius Caesar was besieging the walled city of Marseilles (France). His men first built a brick tower, with a roof that was raised as the tower rose higher by a clever pulley system. From this tower, archers fired through loopholes to cover engineers who were pushing a wooden tunnel on rollers up against the city wall. Inside this shelter, covered by tiles, rope mats and ox-hides to keep off enemy fire, the engineers dug at the wall, until part of it collapsed. Then the city's defenders surrendered.

Towers and tortoises

To climb high walls, the Romans built wooden towers on wheels. Soldiers climbed up ladders inside the tower, and then ran across a ramp onto the enemy wall.

To knock holes in a wall, soldiers dug holes and lit fires to dislodge or crack the stones. To smash down gates, they thumped away with wooden battering rams, with iron-tipped points, until the gate splintered.

The enemy tried to shoot down from the walls to keep the Romans away. For protection, soldiers formed the shield-formation known as the *testudo* or 'tortoise'. The men joined up in rows, forming a roof and walls with their shields. The 'tortoise' then marched forwards. Spears, stones and arrows bounced harmlessly off its shield-shell. It was so strong that (in training) a chariot could be driven over the top!

Roman soldiers sheltering beneath their shields, in the *testudo* – another scene from Trajan's Column. At the top of the picture the enemy soldiers hurl rocks and other missiles, which bounce off the shell of the 'tortoise'.

Fortresses of Rome

Across the Roman **Empire** was a chain of fortresses. These were military bases and centres of government for the Roman **provinces**. **Legions** were based in the biggest fortresses.

Frontier forts

The Romans built a long line of forts and walls to defend their frontiers along the Rhine and Danube rivers. This northern defence line was called the Limes, and along it were army posts like the Saalburg Fort near Frankfurt in Germany. Like most Roman forts, it was rectangular in shape, with the buildings inside resembling a small town. The soldiers lived and ate in **barrack** blocks. At the Saalburg barracks, a **centurion** had his own room while the eighty or so men in his unit shared the other ten rooms in the L-shaped building.

All Roman forts were built to roughly the same pattern, so newly arrived soldiers felt at home. The main buildings included the headquarters where the legion's eagle and **standards** were kept, and the residence of the commanding officer (the **legate**). Along the main street were officers' houses. As well as barracks, the fort had grain stores, workshops (carpenters, blacksmiths, shoemakers, armourers and others) and a hospital. Cavalrymen's horses were stabled inside the fort too. In the legion office, army clerks filed records written in ink on thin shavings of wood, and made lists on wax tablets.

This is the restored Roman fort in Saalburg, Germany. It formed part of the Limes – the empire's northern defences.

A Roman army toilet block, from Hadrian's Wall in north Britain. Water for the toilets came from streams and stone rainwater tanks, or from wells in places where the ground was soft enough to dig through. In remote places like this, the soldiers probably used local moss as wash-sponges.

Baths and toilets

Bathing was an important part of Roman life. Some bath buildings were as long as a medieval cathedral. Though only ruins remain, they show that Roman baths were luxurious, more so than some modern swimming pools! The soldiers could work up a sweat in exercise halls, swim in an outdoor pool, then enjoy hot and cold plunge baths, and a massage. Nothing was too good for a soldier of the Empire!

Latrines (toilets) were in separate buildings. There were wooden planks with seat holes, and a gutter with flowing water to wash the sponges on sticks that the soldiers used for toilet paper.

Working soldiers

Every Roman soldier marched with digging tools and stakes, so he could quickly build a night-camp when on the move. When a new fort was being built, soldiers cleared the site, dug out the foundations, and made the bricks and roof tiles from clay. Soldiers were always busy in and around the fort repairing the walls, cleaning kit and weapons, digging ditches, and preparing food. Soldiers on guard at night kept their eyes open – the punishment for sleeping on watch was death! After a victory, troops might also have to house and guard prisoners of war.

Guarding the frontiers

By AD 100 the Roman **Empire** was at its biggest extent. Its natural **frontiers** were the Atlantic Ocean in the west, the forests and mountains of northern Europe, and the deserts of Africa and Arabia to the south and east. Land frontiers defended by forts marked the edges of the Roman world. Outside lived enemies and **barbarians**. Half the Roman army guarded these frontiers, to defend Rome. There were fifteen legions along the Rhine and Danube to keep out the barbarians, but only one legion in more peaceful North Africa. Policing the borders was a big part of the army's job.

In AD 122, the **emperor** Hadrian visited Britain, shortly after the Romans had put down a fairly serious rebellion. Hadrian decided to build a frontier wall to divide Roman Britain from the un-Roman north (modern Scotland). With him came a legion new to Britain, the Sixth, and its soldiers set to work, with those of the Second Legion and others, to build the wall.

What the wall is like

Hadrian's Wall took eight years to build. It was built from local materials, mainly stones in the east and turf in the west. The height of the wall varied, from 4 to 7 metres, and the top was wide enough for troops to walk along. At intervals there were gates in the wall, to control trade and travel across the frontier, and these gates were protected by walled forts, now known as milecastles. In places the wall had a deep ditch in front of it; elsewhere the ground was so steep a ditch was not needed.

Part of Hadrian's Wall as it looks today. Much of this Roman military wall still winds across the hills of northern England, from the River Solway in the west to the River Tyne in the east, a distance of 118 kilometres (73 miles).

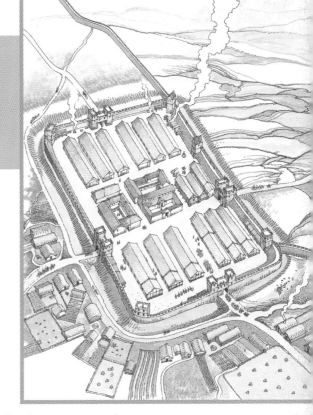

An artist's drawing of what Housesteads Fort on Hadrian's Wall probably looked like. Notice the gate-towers at the entrances, and the headquarters building in the centre. The soldiers lived in the long barracks blocks.

Soldiers on the wall

The legions built the wall, but did not stay to guard it. That job was taken by **auxiliaries**. Some of these soldiers came from sunny southern Europe, and found the weather in northern Britain cold and wet. They wrote letters home, asking for gifts of warm clothes. In winter, the men huddled around open fires in their draughty **barrack** huts; only a fort commander relaxed in a house kept warm by hot air circulating under the floor and through the walls from the *hypocaust*, the Roman central heating system.

The Romans built other frontier walls, but none of these has survived as well as Hadrian's Wall. In AD 142, the Romans built a smaller wall in Britain, between the Forth and Clyde rivers in Scotland. Called the Antonine Wall, after the emperor Antoninus, it was later abandoned.

There was not much fighting around Hadrian's Wall, though at one fort charred timber shows where the Britons tried to set fire to the gates. The forts became 'police stations', the soldiers married local women, and settlements grew up around the forts.

What the soldiers left

Among the things the Romans left behind at Hadrian's Wall are small altars to gods. One found near Carlisle was dedicated to the god 'Jupiter, Best and Greatest' from the 'First German Mixed Battalion'. A tombstone found at the Sixth Legion's base at York was set up by a soldier in memory of his dead child: 'Simplicia Forentina, a most innocent being, who lived ten months'.

Controlling the sea

Rome depended on trade. Grain ships brought food from Egypt and Africa to feed the people. From Roman pictures and from remains of ships found by **archaeologists**, we know that Roman **merchant ships** were broad and fat, with a single sail, and a stern post that curved upwards, like a swan's neck. Some were over 50 metres long. The remains of even bigger ships, around 80 metres long, were discovered in 1932 in Lake Nemi, near Rome. These two giant ships may have been used in mock battles to entertain the emperor.

A **relief** carving of a Roman war galley. This may show Emperor Augustus's flagship, which fought at the Battle of Actium in 31 BC. The ship had a ram sticking out in front and a castle-like structure for soldiers to fight from as it crashed into an enemy ship. It would have had two or three banks of oars.

Copying the best

Until their first war with Carthage in 264 BC, the Romans had no real warships. The Carthaginians were the best shipbuilders of the Mediterranean Sea. After capturing a Carthaginian galley, the Romans took it apart and studied it. Then they built copies for their own navy. The Roman navy used fast galleys for battles and for chasing pirates, and slower transports for moving troops and equipment. In 55 BC, Julius Caesar used 80 ships to carry two legions from **Gaul** (France) to attack Britain. A smaller fleet of eighteen ships carried the **cavalry**.

Roman warships

Warships protected merchant ships from pirates and enemy **fleets**. Like the galleys of ancient Greece, Roman warships were oared ships with two or three banks of oars. The ship was long and slim, best suited to calm seas and shallow inlets. Sticking out from the pointed prow (front end) was a metal-covered ram, for smashing into other ships. The ship had one big main sail, with a smaller sail near the front. It relied on oars when there was no wind, and when going into battle.

The Roman navy was run by a board of officials. There were two main fleets for the defence of Italy and other fleets based at key ports in the Black Sea, the Adriatic, at Alexandria in Egypt, Crete and Britain. A body of soldiers, whom we would call marines, were trained to fight at sea.

Using the navy

Generals used the navy to win fame and influence. Pompey the Great (106–148 BC), promised the **Senate** in Rome that he would clear pirates from the Mediterranean in three months. His rival, Julius Caesar, led a huge fleet to Britain, without ever seriously trying to conquer the island.

Rowing into battle

The calm Mediterranean Sea was ideal for oared ships. The biggest Roman ships had 170 oars. Each ship also carried between 100 and 120 soldiers, who fought on the deck, while the oarsmen sat beneath them. An opening near the front of the ship let in fresh air to cool the sweating men at the long oars.

Life below decks

Roman rowers were not all slaves, like those of other ancient navies, but life below deck in the gloom and smells of the ship's 'engine room' must have been grim. The rowers heaved on the long wooden oars – two men to an oar on the top banks, one man to an oar below. Their ship was so narrow that there was little room for stores or sleeping space. The rowers could rest when the wind filled the big sail, driving the ship along. When the ship went into battle, they went to work.

This coin has a Roman galley warship stamped onto it, like the galleys that fought at Actium. It has a curved prow, a pointed ram and is driven by oars and a large square sail. On deck, marines line up, ready to do battle.

The Battle of Actium

This sea battle was fought off
the coast of Greece in 31 BC.
On one side was a Roman fleet
led by Octavian; on the other the
combined Roman and Egyptian
fleets of Mark Antony and Cleopatra,
Queen of Egypt. The battle ended
when Cleopatra's ships sailed away.
Most of Antony's ships surrendered
to Octavian, who with a huge fleet
of over 700 ships became master of
the Roman world. He later became
the first **emperor** Augustus. Antony
and Cleopatra fled to Egypt, where
they both committed suicide.

GREECE

Ionian
Sea

Actium

0   50 miles
0   80 km

- Octavian's fleet
- Cleopatra's fleet
- Mark Antony's fleet

Into battle

In a battle, the rowers' job was to drive the ship at top speed
towards a collision! As two fleets drew closer, each captain steered
his ship at an enemy ship, with the rowers straining every muscle
for top speed. He tried to ram the enemy vessel, smash a hole in
its side, and then draw back, leaving it to sink. All the while,
catapults and *ballistas* fired stones and giant arrows, and lobbed
balls of burning tar onto the wooden decks. Arrows and javelins
flew between the ships, and sailors used long iron hooks to tear
down the enemy's mast and sail. When two ships finally crashed
together, the Romans lowered an assault ramp and charged across
to fight hand-to-hand with swords, spears and axes.

Fireships

Fire could be a deadly weapon at sea. Blazing fireships were used
to set fire to enemy ships in harbour. With the wind blowing from
behind them, the Romans would pack old ships with wood, tar and
oil-soaked rags, and set them on fire. The wind took the fireships
towards the enemy, causing havoc and confusion.

Rome victorious

For over 200 years, victory seemed to follow victory. The Roman soldier seemed unbeatable. Many peoples accepted Roman rule, and enjoyed the Roman way of life. Everywhere the Romans went, they built Roman towns, ports, roads, temples and farms. The Roman soldier carried a spade as well as a sword, and the Romans were usually as good at making peace as they were at waging war.

The Arch of Constantine in Rome was erected in AD 312 to mark the emperor Constantine's victory over his rival Maxentius. The work was done in a hurry, which is why the builders included bits of sculpture from earlier buildings, with battle scenes and pictures of prisoners taken in wars fought by earlier emperors.

Trajan's wars

The Emperor Trajan was born in Spain, in about AD 53. Emperor Nerva chose this tough soldier as the next emperor, and Trajan took over in AD 98, after Nerva died. Trajan's armies conquered Dacia (a land in what is now Romania/Hungary), and Nabatea (a kingdom covering parts of modern Jordan and Saudi Arabia). Trajan's Column in Rome was built in his honour. The 30-metre-high pillar is decorated with carvings showing Roman soldiers in Dacia. Trajan died in AD 117.

Resistance and revenge

After a rare defeat, Roman revenge could be savage. In AD 66, the Jews of Judea revolted and drove out their Roman masters. Four years later, the Roman **general** Titus captured Jerusalem and destroyed the Jewish Temple. Many Jews were taken as captives to Rome. A small band of Jews refused to surrender and retreated to a mountain stronghold called Masada. There 960 men, women and children fought off a Roman army for three years, and in the end killed themselves rather than be made slaves.

Roman triumph

From **Gaul** in the west to Palestine in the east, Roman armies stood guard. Thirty-four **arsenal** cities across the **Empire** supplied these armies with equipment and weapons. By the AD 200s, there were at least 500,000 soldiers of Rome.

Proud of such military might, the Romans expected their **emperors** to provide them with victories and victory parades. The Romans celebrated victory with processions that could last three days. Captive kings in chains, strange weapons, and statues of gods taken from foreign temples: all were dragged through Rome. Loot was also paraded. Thousands of slaves staggered through the streets, carrying armfuls of coins, gold and silver, and precious stones. A hundred white oxen would be led to the temple, as a sacrifice to the gods. Drums pounded, trumpets blared, and crowds cheered a successful general.

Decline and fall of the Roman army

The **emperor** Diocletian doubled the size of the army in the AD 280s. This was a sign that Rome was in trouble. More soldiers were needed to protect the Roman **Empire** from its enemies. Unfortunately, there were more weak emperors than strong ones like Diocletian, and **frontier provinces** were increasingly left to defend themselves. Great fortresses began to crumble. The Pax Romana (Latin for 'Roman peace') was no more.

Constantine moves to the East

Rome's first Christian emperor was Constantine, who won his battle for power in AD 312 after seeing (he said) a vision of Christ. He told his soldiers to wear a symbol of Jesus on their shields. Constantine moved his capital east, to the city of Byzantium, renamed Constantinople (modern Istanbul in Turkey). He set up a 'mobile reserve'; an army ready at any time to march to the aid of the frontier **legions**.

Constantine was known as 'the Great', and he ruled from c.AD 280–337. This enormous sculpture of Constantine's head dates from the 4th century AD and is from the Forum in Rome.

The Roman legion was smaller now, about 2000 men, and less important than the **cavalry**, but not even cavalry could fight off so many **barbarians**. The empire had grown too big to defend. From AD 364 it was divided, with separate emperors ruling the Eastern and Western halves.

The end of the Western Empire

The Romans now hired their enemies as **mercenaries**. In Britain, the army built coastal forts such as Pevensey Castle in Sussex, and manned a fleet of ships to fight off raiding Saxons (from north-west Europe). The British got little help from Rome. In the end, they had to pay Saxons to fight for them.

By AD 410, the frontier forts could no longer keep out thousands of German invaders, who streamed across the River Rhine into Roman **Gaul**. Britain's last remaining Roman soldiers hurriedly left the island, to fight the Germans. However it was hopeless. In AD 410, Rome was captured by an army of Goths (Germanic people) led by Alaric. In AD 451, Romans and barbarians in western Europe joined forces, to fight an army of eastern Huns led by Attila. Finally in 476 a German ruler named Odoacer overthrew the last Roman emperor and made himself king of Italy. The Roman armies were no more. Only in the Eastern Empire, ruled from Byzantium, did some Roman ways continue.

Last battle of the legions

The last great battle of the Roman legions was fought in AD 378 at Adrianople, (modern Edirne in Turkey). An army led by the Eastern emperor Valens was overrun by hordes of Goths, whose cavalry shattered the Roman foot-soldiers. Valens and over 40,000 Romans were killed. The new emperor Theodosius was forced to hand over food to the Goths, in return for their military service.

How do we know?

We know about the Romans at war from the accounts of **generals**, such as Julius Caesar, and from the writings of **historians** such as the Roman Tacitus and the Jewish writer Josephus. Josephus for example describes how the Roman army marched as it advanced to attack the Jews.

The clearest pictures we have of Roman warriors and their weapons come from tombstones and from Trajan's Column. This famous monument in Rome was finished in AD 113, after seven years' work. It stands 38 metres (125 feet) high, and around it runs a spiral band over a metre (4 feet) wide and 240 metres (800 feet) long. This band is a picture-strip carved in **relief** telling the story of Roman soldiers at war in Dacia, under Trajan's command. The carvings on Trajan's Column show the clothing and kit of soldiers, and the way they fought on campaign.

What archaeologists look for

Many Roman army camps and other Roman settlements have been excavated by **archaeologists**. From such sites, archaeologists and **historians** build up a picture of Roman life – weapons, food, clothing and so on. Oyster shells, beef and codfish bones, and cherry and plum stones give clues as to what the Romans ate. Other finds include coins, scraps of shoes, millstones (for grinding grain into flour), metal tools and broken pottery.

This towering pillar of stone is Trajan's Column in Rome. It is one of the best records of the Romans at war.

Along Hadrian's Wall, the Romans put in marker stones at intervals, to say which soldiers had built which section. The writing on this stone tells us that century Florinus (that is, the 80 or so men in the Florinus century) added a section of wall 22 paces long.

Sites that tell a story

Frontier sites such as Hadrian's Wall in northern England and forts such as Caerleon in Wales and Saalburg in Germany provide more evidence. The Roman cities of Herculaneum and Pompeii, buried by a volcano eruption in AD 79, also give a vivid picture of life in Roman times.

More long-buried evidence is sometimes found during city rebuilding. Much of Roman London, for example, came to light as builders went to work in bombed areas after the Second World War (1939-45). The remains of the Roman fort in London were discovered and also a temple dedicated to Mithras, a favourite god among Roman soldiers.

The Romans' achievement

The Romans were good soldiers, but even better organizers. Other warriors were as brave, but few were so methodical or determined. When told that his enemy's stronghold could last out a **siege** of ten years, a Roman commander replied 'then we will capture it in the 11th year'. The Romans could be cruel and ruthless, but on the whole their **Empire** was governed well. People under Roman rule prospered, and for over 500 years the Roman army kept much of Europe and the Mediterranean world at peace – no small achievement.

Timeline

BC

753	Traditional date for the founding of the city of Rome
c.510	Romans revolt against Etruscan rule
200	Rome by now rules all Italy
146	Greece and Macedonia become Roman provinces
82	Sulla uses army to try to win power
55	Julius Caesar lands in Britain for the first time
44	Julius Caesar is murdered
31	Octavian wins sea battle of Actium, defeating Antony and Cleopatra

AD

43	Claudius orders army to invade Britain.
79	Vesuvius erupts, and buries Roman cities of Pompeii and Herculaneum
90	Vindolanda fort in Northumberland built
101–107	Romans conquer Dacia, and the empire reaches its greatest size
106–113	Trajan's Column set up in Rome
122	Hadrian orders the building of a wall to defend northern Britain
142	Romans build Antonine Wall in Scotland
364	Roman Empire is finally divided into separate empires, East (Rome) and West (Constantinople)
410	Last Roman soldiers leave Britain – Roman-British people are left to defend themselves
476	Last Roman emperor in the West is overthrown by Goths.

Sources and further reading

Sources

Daily Life in Ancient Rome,
Florence Dupont (Blackwell, 1992)
The English Heritage Book of Villas and the Roman Countryside,
Guy de la Bedoyere (English Heritage/Batsford 1993)
The Great Invasion,
Leonard Cottrell (Evans Brothers, 1958)
Greece and Rome at War,
Peter Connolly (Macdonald, 1981)
Roman Britain,
Peter Salway (Oxford University Press, 1992)
Roman Britain,
H. H. Scullard (Thames and Hudson, 1994)
The Roman Invasion of Britain,
Graham Webster (Batsford, 1993)
Roman London,
Hall and Merrifield (HMSO/Museum of London, 1986)
Roman Towns in Britain,
Guy de la Bedoyere (English Heritage/Batsford 1992)
Women in Roman Britain,
Lindsay Allason-Jones (British Museum, 1989)

Further reading

Ancient Rome,
Mike Corbishley (Facts on File/Equinox, 1989)
Family Life in Roman Britain,
Peter Chrisp (Hodder Wayland, 2001)
Look Inside a Roman Villa,
Peter Chrisp (Hodder Wayland, 2002)
Roman Villas and Great Houses,
Brenda Williams (Heinemann, 1997)
What Happened Here?: Roman Palace,
Tim Wood (A & C Black, 2000)

Glossary

allies friends, people who agree to work or fight as members of an alliance

Alps large range of mountains in Europe to the north of Italy

ambush surprise attack by an enemy in hiding

archaeologist expert on the past, who studies objects and evidence underground or beneath the sea

arsenal place where weapons are made and stored

artillery weapons for firing missiles

auxiliary soldier who was not a Roman citizen, usually from the provinces

barbarian non-Roman, usually an enemy; to Romans, anyone who did not speak Latin was a barbarian

barracks building where soldiers live and sleep

cast describes an object made from hot metal poured into a mould

cavalry soldiers on horseback

Celts peoples living across Europe, in different tribes

centurion officer roughly equivalent to a sergeant in a modern army, in charge of a century (between 80 and 100 men)

citizen Roman man who was entitled to vote in elections and serve in the legions

civilian someone who is not a soldier

civil war fighting between two groups within one country

crucified being hung on a cross, a form of execution in Roman times

drill practising marching and obeying orders

emperor supreme ruler of Rome; the first ruler to hold the Latin title *imperator* was Augustus

empire large area with many peoples living under rule of an emperor

Etruscans people who controlled central Italy before the Romans

fleet group of warships

frontier boundary between Roman-ruled territory and another

Gaul Roman province, covering large part of western Europe (modern France, Belgium and southern Germany)

general commander of an army

hill-fort fort-settlement built by Celts in Britain

historian someone who writes about past events and people

infantry foot soldiers

legate commander of a legion and governor of a province

legion main battle unit of the Roman army, numbering at various times between 4000 and 6000 soldiers called **legionaries**

mail armour made from interlocking metal rings, rather like a flexible coat

merchant ship ship for carrying cargo, such as food or trade goods

mercenaries hired soldiers, fighting for money

missile object thrown through the air, such a spear, stone or arrow

mule animal, a cross between a horse and a donkey

phalanx Greek army formation of foot soldiers with long spears

provinces territories conquered and ruled by Romans, such as *Britannia* (Britain) and *Gallia* (Gaul)

relief picture carved in stone to give a three-dimensional effect

republic form of government in early Rome, with elected officials, not a king

scabbard holder or sheath for a sword

scouts soldiers sent ahead of the army to look out for enemies

Senate Rome's parliament, made up of important people and former officials, who advised the elected consuls

siege attack on a fort or city, surrounded by an army outside

standard ceremonial pole of a legion, carried into battle by a standard-bearer

surveyor person who planned routes of Roman roads

treaties agreements made between countries or rulers

tunic shirt-like garment which came down to just above the knee

veterans retired soldiers

winch wheel and rope machine, turned by handles

Index